Let Freedom Ring

Robert E. Lee

by Judy Monroe

Consultant:
J. Holt Merchant, Professor of History
Washington and Lee University
Lexington, Virginia

Bridgestone Books
an imprint of Capstone Press
Mankato, Minnesota

Bridgestone Books are published by Capstone Press,
151 Good Counsel Drive • P.O. Box 669 • Mankato, Minnesota 56002.
www.capstonepress.com

Printed in the United States of America

Library of Congress Cataloging-in-Publication Data
Monroe, Judy.
    Robert E. Lee / by Judy Monroe.
        p. cm. — (Let freedom ring)
    Includes bibliographical references and index.
    ISBN 0-7386-1089-7 (hardcover)
    ISBN 0-7386-4525-9 (paperback)
    1. Lee, Robert E. (Robert Edward), 1807–1870—Juvenile literature. 2. Generals—
Confederate States of America—Biography—Juvenile literature. 3. Confederate States of
America. Army—Biography—Juvenile literature. [1. Lee, Robert E. (Robert Edward),
1807–1870. 2. Generals. 3. Confederate States of America. 4. United States—History—Civil
War, 1861–1865.] I. Title. II. Series.
E467.1.L4 M65 2002
973.7'3'092—dc21   2001003059
                                                                          CIP

Summary: Traces the family life and military career of Robert E. Lee, before, during, and
    after the U.S. Civil War.

Editorial Credits

Charles Pederson, editor; Kia Bielke, cover designer, interior layout designer, and illustrator;
Deirdre Barton, photo researcher

Photo Credits

CORBIS, cover, 16, 25, 29, 35, 36; Hulton/Archive, 5, 15, 21 (top), 33; Lee Snider/CORBIS,
7, 42; Joseph Sohm, ChromoSohm Inc./CORBIS, 8; Gary Sundermeyer/Capstone Press, 10;
N. Carter/North Wind Pictures Archive, 11; North Wind Pictures, 13; Stock Montage, Inc.,
19, 41; Buddy Mays/CORBIS, 21 (bottom); Smithsonian American Art Museum,
Washington, D.C./Art Resource, 22; Art Resource, 31, 39

1   2   3   4   5   6   07   06   05   04   03   02

Table of Contents

Chapter One

Military Hero and More

Some people have called Robert E. Lee the United States' "very best soldier." Robert was a brilliant military leader who got the best from his soldiers, yet he thought he would never lead in battle.

Robert's military background was varied. He fought in the Mexican War (1846–1848). He later used that experience in the U.S. Civil War (1861–1865). This war was four long years of Americans fighting Americans.

Robert displayed bold and clever military knowledge. War experts call him a genius. Yet Robert never wanted civil war. When it began, he had to choose to fight for the North, the Union, or for the South, the Confederacy. In deciding, he said he wept "tears of blood."

Robert may not have won the war for his side. Yet his military genius earned him a hero's place in history. His sense of honor and duty earned him the nation's respect.

Many people consider Robert E. Lee to be one of the best military commanders in U.S. history. He was much more than that, however.

Chapter Two

The Young Virginian

Robert Edward Lee was born on January 19, 1807, at Stratford Hall, a large house in Westmoreland County, Virginia. Robert was one of seven children of Harry "Light Horse" Lee and Ann Carter Lee.

Robert's father, Harry, was a governor of Virginia. He fought in the American Revolutionary War (1775–1783). General George Washington praised Harry's daring and skill in battles.

Harry's skills at war did not help run a home, however, and he did not manage money well. When Robert was a baby, Harry made some bad land deals. When he could not repay the money he lost on the deals, he spent a year in jail. Around this time, the Lees moved to Alexandria, Virginia.

In 1813, Harry sailed to the West Indies, islands south of America. Robert was 6 and never saw his father again. Harry died in 1818 when he tried to return home.

Robert E. Lee was born at Stratford Hall, in Virginia (above). He fondly remembered his childhood years here.

Growing Up

After Harry's death, Ann carefully managed the family home and slaves and reared the children. She loved her children deeply and took good care of them. Robert's mother taught him much about money management, duty, and love of family.

Ann became ill when Robert was 13 years old. She probably had tuberculosis, a serious lung disease. Robert's other brothers had left home, and Robert was the only son living with his mother. He read to his mother, gave her medicines, and took

These cadets are marching at the present-day U.S. Military Academy. Their uniforms are like the ones Robert and the other cadets wore at the school.

her for rides in their carriage. He began to manage the household.

Robert was a good student who studied hard and earned good grades. His homework was never late. Math was his favorite class.

In 1823, Robert finished school and needed to earn a living. He decided to study to become a soldier and engineer. Engineers need strong math skills to design bridges, waterways, and machines.

At age 18, Robert entered the United States Military Academy at West Point, New York. His life at the academy began in June 1825.

Academy Life

Life at the academy was strictly scheduled. Students, called cadets, rose early each morning. They marched before breakfast in all weather. After breakfast, they went to classes for seven hours.

After dinner, cadets followed a routine, too. They studied until 9:00 at night. Each evening, lights went out at 10:00 to end the day. The same routine began the next morning. The cadets had some free time only on Sunday afternoons, Christmas Day, and New Year's Day.

In those days, the head of the academy kept a book with pages set aside for each cadet. The academy head kept a record of demerits, or points off for breaking rules. Robert never received a single demerit. His record still stands today. By Robert's third year, his page was used for another cadet who kept getting into trouble.

Robert wanted to follow the military example of his father. Many people respected Harry for his military skill. Robert wanted the same respect from his fellow Virginians.

Engineering and Marriage

Robert did well in all his classes, especially engineering. He studied other subjects such as math, French, drawing, and military planning. Robert graduated second in his class in June 1829.

Because of his outstanding grades, Robert was assigned to an

engineering unit of the U.S. Army. While Robert waited to find out where he would work, he visited his mother, who was ill and dying. He stayed with her until she died a few weeks later.

The army sent Robert to help build Fort Pulaski, on Cockspur Island, a swampy island off the coast of Savannah, Georgia. The work moved slowly in the hot, muddy area. Robert helped dig a moat around the fort. This water-filled ditch protected the fort during attacks.

Robert's first job was at Fort Pulaski (left) in Georgia. A moat surrounded the fort.

In his spare time, Robert visited nearby relatives. He fell in love with Mary Anne Randolph Custis, a distant relative. Robert asked Mary to marry him. She accepted, and they married on June 30, 1831.

Work Goes On

The U.S. Army ordered Robert to go to St. Louis, Missouri, on the Mississippi River. He had to figure out how to change the river's flow to keep sand from filling a government dock area. His idea was to build a dike so the river would wash away the sand.

In 1841, the army sent Robert to Fort Hamilton in Brooklyn, New York. He was in charge of repairing the forts that guarded New York Harbor.

By age 39, Robert had never seen fighting and was not a hero like his father. Yet he still dreamed of leading troops in battle. His chance came in 1846 when the United States declared war on Mexico. The army ordered Robert to join this war.

The Lee Children

Robert's family often stayed at the family home, Arlington House (below). The house was set on a hill in Virginia, across the Potomac River from Washington, D.C.

Robert loved his three boys and four girls. He joked and played with them. He liked to tell them stories and let them tickle him. He expected his children to behave well and to be clean and neat.

When away, Robert wrote to his wife and children. In one letter, he said: "You do not know how much I have missed you and the children, my dear Mary." Robert wanted his children to do their best. He wrote that the children "*can* if they try & I say in addition they *Must*."

Chapter Three

At War with Mexico

In 1845, U.S. president James K. Polk tried to buy present-day California and New Mexico. At that time, Mexico owned the area, which made up almost half of all Mexico. The Mexican government did not want to sell such a large part of its territory.

Mexico was angry that Texas had become part of the United States. Mexico wanted to regain control over Texas. On April 25, 1846, the Mexican army attacked American troops along the Rio Grande. This river marked the border of Texas and Mexico. On May 13, the U.S. Congress declared war on Mexico. The Mexican War had started.

Many people disagreed with the reasons for the war. Some people felt that the United States was picking on a smaller country. But Robert was eager to see war action. So when the army sent him to San Antonio, Texas, he went.

U.S. President James Polk (above) tried to buy land from Mexico, which refused to sell. The U.S. government went to war to gain the land.

By September 1846, Robert reached General John Wool's soldiers, who were preparing to move to the Rio Grande. The United States considered the river to be the southern border of Texas, but Mexico believed the border was farther east. Wool's troops were to cross the Rio Grande and invade northern Mexico.

Robert acted as scout for the engineering teams that improved roads and built bridges. Thousands of army men hauled heavy guns along these roads and bridges. Robert and his men chose and set up camp for the troops each night.

At right, the Mexican Army sails the Rio Grande in the 1840s. The area north of the river was a source of tensions that led to the Mexican War.

Several times, Robert explored enemy territory. Through this risky and dangerous work, Robert was able to provide useful information to Wool. The general was pleased with Robert's courage and ideas. He promoted Robert to acting inspector general of his army.

The Planner

The army next sent Robert to the Gulf Coast in Mexico. There, General Winfield Scott was planning to attack Vera Cruz, a large port city. Thousands of American soldiers had landed near Vera Cruz in early March 1847. Scott ordered Robert to get the big army guns ready to attack the city.

Robert told his men where to dig ditches and set up the heavy guns. Under Robert's direction, the work went smoothly. Within two days, all was ready, and the shelling began. The guns soon won Vera Cruz for the Americans.

Scott was pleased with Robert's planning. He called Robert to his tent to figure out how to cross enemy land to attack Mexico City, the Mexican capital.

Known as a good scout, Robert proved himself again. He scouted a way to cross the dangerous pedregal, a large, rough lava bed near Mexico City. Robert crossed this rocky area not once, but three times. Scott called Robert's scouting trips "the greatest feat of physical and mental courage." Robert's engineers built a road across the pedregal. Scott and his men safely crossed the area and marched toward Mexico City.

The End of the Mexican War

Capturing Mexico City was the final goal, but Chapultepec, Mexico's strongest fort, blocked the way. Robert planned a way to storm the rough hill.

Robert guided the first troops to the fort on September 13, 1847. By now, Robert had been awake for hours, but his excitement kept him going. During the fighting, a bullet struck Robert. He was not seriously injured, but while he recovered, his army captured Chapultepec. The way to Mexico City was free, and American troops entered the city.

Mexico surrendered on September 14, 1847. In early 1848, Mexico and America signed a peace treaty. Mexico agreed that Texas belonged to the United States. Mexico also sold California, New Mexico, Nevada, Utah, and Arizona to the United States for about $15 million.

In just over five months, Scott's army had done what many thought impossible. He had defeated Mexico and captured its capital. Scott gave much credit to the newly promoted Colonel Lee. General Scott praised Robert's bravery. The Mexican War taught Robert much about battle. He soon used the knowledge in the Civil War.

General Winfield Scott was pleased with Robert's military skill during the Mexican War.

Chapter Four

The Road to Civil War

After the Mexican War, Robert returned to his family as a hero. He had been gone nearly two years, however, and looked older. When he walked into his home, only his little dog, Spec, recognized him. Soon, however, his children again played games with Robert and listened to his stories. Robert and Mary spent time together.

Robert focused again on engineering projects. From 1849 to 1852, Robert did engineering work at Fort Carroll in Baltimore, Maryland. Mary and the children traveled between Baltimore and Arlington.

In 1852, the U.S. Army ordered Robert to lead the United States Military Academy. Robert did not want to be in charge of the academy. Still, the army thought he was the best man for the job, so Robert obeyed.

The top picture shows cadets and cannons at the military academy at West Point about 1861. In 1852, Robert became the leader of the academy.

In 1855, Robert was promoted to lieutenant colonel and sent to Texas to protect settlers from the Comanche Indians. He did not fight the Comanches but simply patrolled a wide area of dusty Texas land. He missed his family, who stayed at Arlington House.

This painting shows a Comanche village in about 1835. Robert was sent to protect Texas settlers from Comanche warriors.

Family Business

In 1857, Robert went home. Mary's father, George Washington Parke Custis, recently had died. Robert stayed two years to work out the will of Mary's father. Custis had owned a plantation and slaves. Plantations grow one main crop. Custis owed $10,000. Robert was supposed to pay the bills and then free Custis's slaves.

Custis had not taken care of the plantation. Robert put the slaves to work painting buildings, repairing roofs, and plowing and planting the fields.

A New York newspaper heard that Robert was making slaves work when he should have freed them. The newspaper called him cruel for owning slaves. Robert did not respond.

In the mid-1800s, the issue of slavery divided America. Some people in the South used slaves to work their farms. Many people in the North were against slavery.

John Brown Fights Slavery

John Brown was a U.S. citizen who strongly opposed slavery and believed he needed to free slaves. Brown

Slavery and Robert

Robert believed slavery was wrong. In 1856, he wrote Mary that slavery was "evil." But Robert believed that slaves could not take care of themselves and needed their owners to provide food, clothing, and shelter. Robert thought that slaves should be set free gradually. Like many white people of that time, Robert thought African Americans should not have equal rights.

had worked against slavery and come to believe that only violence would succeed in stopping it.

In mid-October 1859, Brown gathered 21 armed men and entered the town of Harpers Ferry, Virginia. In the town stood an arsenal where the federal, or central, government stored some of its guns. Some people believe that Brown planned to set up a safe base in the nearby mountains for slaves. Then he wanted to lead a large group north through the mountains to freedom.

On October 16, 1859, Brown and his men captured the arsenal and 13 men. Local soldiers soon surrounded the arsenal. The soldiers were unsure of what to do next.

The federal government ordered Robert along with U.S. troops to take back the Harpers Ferry arsenal. He was to arrest John Brown.

On the morning of October 18, Robert's soldiers surrounded the arsenal. Robert asked Brown to surrender, but Brown refused. Robert ordered his soldiers to break into the arsenal and capture Brown and his men. During their two days in the firehouse, 10 of Brown's people died,

John Brown (left) believed that only armed violence would end slavery. In 1859, he led 21 men in a revolution against the U.S. government.

including two of Brown's sons. Robert finally captured Brown, who was hanged on December 2. No slaves joined Brown's army.

America Splits Apart

Many states had already declared themselves to be slave states or nonslave states. Brown's actions increased tensions between proslavery and antislavery groups.

In 1860, Abraham Lincoln was elected U.S. president. He hated slavery, yet he said it was legal under the Constitution, and the federal government had no power to outlaw it. Each state, he said, could decide whether slavery was legal there. Despite Lincoln's words, many Southerners believed Lincoln would try to end slavery.

On December 20, 1860, South Carolina seceded from the United States. The state did not want as its leader a man who hated slavery, so it left the Union. Soon, 10 states joined South Carolina to form their own country, the Confederate States of America. These states were Mississippi, Florida, Alabama, Georgia, Louisiana, Texas, Virginia,

CANADA

WASHINGTON TERRITORY

OREGON

DAKOTA TERRITORY

MINNESOTA

MICHIGAN

VERMONT

MAINE

NEVADA TERRITORY

UTAH TERRITORY

NEBRASKA TERRITORY

WISCONSIN

IOWA

NEW YORK

NEW HAMPSHIRE

MASSACHUSETTS

COLORADO TERRITORY

KANSAS

MISSOURI

ILLINOIS

INDIANA

OHIO

PENNSYLVANIA

RHODE ISLAND

CONNECTICUT

NEW JERSEY

DELAWARE

MARYLAND

CALIFORNIA

NEW MEXICO TERRITORY

INDIAN TERRITORY

ARKANSAS

KENTUCKY

TENNESSEE

VIRGINIA

NORTH CAROLINA

SOUTH CAROLINA

TEXAS

MISSISSIPPI

ALABAMA

GEORGIA

LOUISIANA

FLORIDA

MEXICO

Miles
0   150   300   450   600

0   500   1000
Kilometers

■ United States (nonslave)

□ Confederate States (slave)

■ Border States (Union states allowing slavery)

□ Territories (neutral)

The North and South in 1861

At the start of the Civil War, the United States had divided into the Union and the Confederacy.

Love of State First

In Robert's time, many people were loyal first to their state, then second, to the United States. This was true even though the Revolutionary War had united the states nearly 90 years earlier.

Though some Southerners did not want to secede, others thought secession a fine idea. Plantation owners depended on slavery for their way of life. They believed the South had the right to form its own government and did not have to give up rights to the federal government. The South believed that each state, and not the federal government, should decide about slavery.

Arkansas, North Carolina, and Tennessee. Jefferson Davis became the president.

Robert Must Decide

The harbor of Charleston, South Carolina, was important to the South. Other countries sent food and supplies through the harbor. Without Fort Sumter, a U.S. fort in the harbor, the Confederacy could not control Charleston. On April 12, 1861,

Confederate troops fired on Fort Sumter. The attack began the Civil War.

Lincoln wanted Robert to command the U.S. Army. Before Robert decided, he met with Winfield Scott. Scott knew that Robert was the army's best officer and wanted him to take command. Scott, like Robert, was from Virginia. He had decided to stay with the Union.

Robert rode to Arlington House to discuss the offer with his family. Robert had been in the army for more than 30 years and was known as a great military leader. His decision would affect the result of the war.

Abraham Lincoln (left) wanted Robert to command the Union Army in the Civil War.

Chapter Five

The Divided Country

By April 20, 1861, Robert had decided to leave the U.S. Army. General Winfield Scott told Robert, "You have made the greatest mistake of your life."

On April 23, Robert accepted a position as a Confederate Army general. He put together an army within weeks. However, Jefferson Davis used Robert as an advisor rather than a leader in battle. Robert created battle plans and organized soldiers, but he really wanted to lead in battle.

By May, Union troops crossed into northern Virginia and seized Arlington House. The federal government used Arlington House as a cemetery for Union dead. Mary Lee and two daughters fled the house to live in Richmond.

Davis sent Robert to defend the coast of South Carolina, Georgia, and Florida. In three months, he had strengthened the area against Union troops.

In March 1862, more than 100,000 Union soldiers marched toward

This portrait of Robert appeared during the Mexican War. It reappeared in 1861, when Robert accepted a position in the Confederate Army.

Uneven Powers

At the start of the Civil War, the South and North were not evenly matched. About 6 million Southerners in 11 states stood against 22 million Northerners in 23 states. About 3 million Southern slaves were not allowed to fight. The North had twice as much railroad and better agriculture than the South. It had many more factories to produce weapons and other materials.

The North, though, did not have Robert's skilled military leadership. This in itself nearly made the warring sides even.

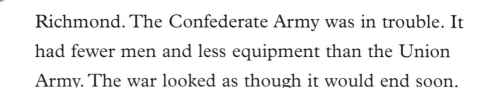

Richmond. The Confederate Army was in trouble. It had fewer men and less equipment than the Union Army. The war looked as though it would end soon.

On May 9, 1862, President Davis ordered his government to leave Richmond. Robert disagreed. "Richmond must not be given up," he said.

Robert Finally Fights

Davis put Robert in command of the Army of Northern Virginia to save Richmond. Robert finally got his wish to lead soldiers in battle.

After months of battles with Union troops, Robert and his soldiers were hungry and tired. Many of his men were dressed in rags. But he believed attacking was better than waiting to be attacked.

In September 1862, Robert led his weary men across the Potomac River toward Antietam Creek, near Sharpsburg, Maryland. His army numbered about 40,000, half as many as the Union soldiers who awaited them.

In 1862, Robert's troops crossed the Potomac River into Maryland. Robert planned to attack the Union Army.

Robert divided his army into four groups and sent them in four directions. He hoped to fool the Union into thinking that his army was large. Union General George B. McClellan learned of Robert's plans. The armies met at the Battle of Antietam on September 17, 1862. Thousands of men died on both sides, and Robert's army withdrew to Virginia.

Freedom for Southern Slaves

After Antietam, President Lincoln decided to issue the Emancipation Proclamation on January 1, 1863. This was an order to free slaves in Confederate-held areas. The border states of Maryland, Kentucky, Missouri, and Delaware had slaves but had remained loyal to the Union. The proclamation did not affect their slaves. It also did not affect some parts of the Confederacy already under Union control.

Lincoln made the proclamation for two reasons. He wanted to end slavery and he wanted to fire up Union troops to defeat the South and save the Union.

Great Victory and Great Loss

In May 1863, Robert won his greatest victory at Chancellorsville, Virginia. He divided his army into three parts. The troops confused the larger Union force when Robert's army attacked. His men drove back the Union troops.

At this battle, Robert suffered a great personal loss. His most trusted general, Thomas Jackson, died soon after the battle. Jackson's own men accidentally shot him after dark. Robert was never as successful after he lost Jackson.

Thomas "Stonewall" Jackson was one of Robert's most trusted generals. His own men accidentally shot and killed him.

Gettysburg: The Turning Point

In the summer of 1863, Robert entered the North again. He crossed the Blue Ridge Mountains and marched up the Shenandoah River. Then he crossed Maryland to Gettysburg, Pennsylvania, where he put his whole army.

On July 1, Robert attacked Union forces at Gettysburg under General George Meade, whose

This painting shows fighting during the Battle of Gettysburg. The battle marked the turning point in the Civil War.

army numbered almost 95,000. The Confederate soldiers numbered about 75,000. For three days, Robert's men fought hard, but they lost the battle. The Union troops were too strong and well organized. On the night of July 4, Robert began a retreat to Virginia.

Losses for the the Union and Confederate armies during the Battle of Gettysburg were huge. The Union army lost about 23,000 soldiers. The Confederates lost about 28,000 soldiers.

The battle was the Civil War's turning point. It marked Robert's last major invasion of the North. He no longer could win by striking first. He had lost so many soldiers that little hope remained of winning the war. Still, he continued to do his best.

The End of War

In 1864, Robert led the Confederates in a series of bloody battles in Virginia against the Northern army. The new Union commander, Ulysses S. Grant, wanted to end the war quickly. Robert fought well against Grant and caused heavy losses in the Union Army. In February 1865, Robert was promoted to General in Chief of all the Confederate troops.

The Cost of Goods

Near the end of the war, the prices of food and other items rose dramatically. Varina Davis, wife of the Confederate president, noted in her diary that turkeys cost $60 each and a man's suit cost $2,700. In 1865, a Richmond clerk named J. B. Jones listed the cost of some items. For example, "A [bed], such as I have bought for $10 [earlier in the war], brought $700."

Robert was forced to defend Richmond and nearby Petersburg, Virginia. Grant finally broke through the Southern lines in April to capture Richmond. By then, Robert's troops had little to eat. Also, there were many more Union than Confederate soldiers.

Robert tried to escape with his army to join other Confederate forces in North Carolina. Grant trapped Robert's army at Appomattox Court House, Virginia, and forced Robert to surrender on April 9, 1865. "I did not

see how a surrender could have been avoided," said Robert. After he surrendered, other Southern armies soon surrendered, too.

The Civil War damaged the nation. About 260,000 Confederate soldiers and about 360,000 Union soldiers had died. Thousands more soldiers were injured. Millions of African Americans were no longer slaves but had no homes or education.

After the war, the U.S. government accused Robert of being a traitor to the Union by making war. The government later dropped the charges.

Robert (seated left) surrendered his army to Ulysses Grant (seated at Robert's left hand) on April 9, 1865.

Chapter Six

Lee's Gifts to Us Today

Robert was a genius at war, but he was much more than that. After the Civil War, he became a symbol of courage and peace. He worked hard to rebuild harmony between the South and North.

On October 2, 1865, Robert became the president of Washington College in Lexington, Virginia. He worked at the college until his death in Lexington on October 12, 1870.

As head of the college, he increased the number of students from 40 to 400 and expanded the kinds of classes offered. He enjoyed teaching young men, too, especially former soldiers, in the ways of peace rather than war. Most importantly, he worked to bring the North and South together again. In Robert's honor, the college was renamed Washington and Lee University.

Robert was a man of gentle courage and iron determination. The country and the world can learn from his example.

After the war, Robert served as president of Washington College. There, he worked hard to heal the wounds between the North and South.

TIMELINE

Robert's Life

Born in
Westmoreland
County, Virginia,
January 19

Married Mary Anne
Randolph Custis

Entered military academy

Father died

Graduated
from academy;
mother died.

| 1807 | 1818 | 1825 | 1829 | 1831 | 1846 | 1847 | 1848 |

Historical Events

Mexican War started.

Battles of Vera Cruz
and Mexico City

Mexican War ended.

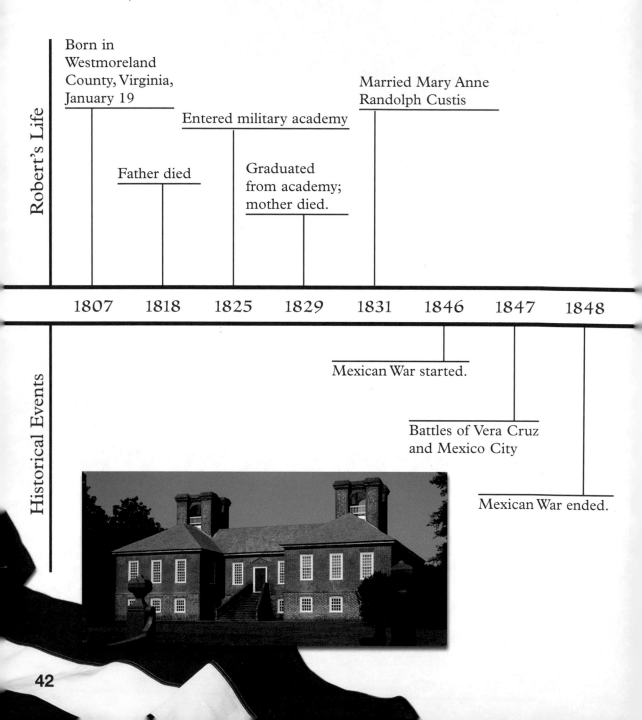

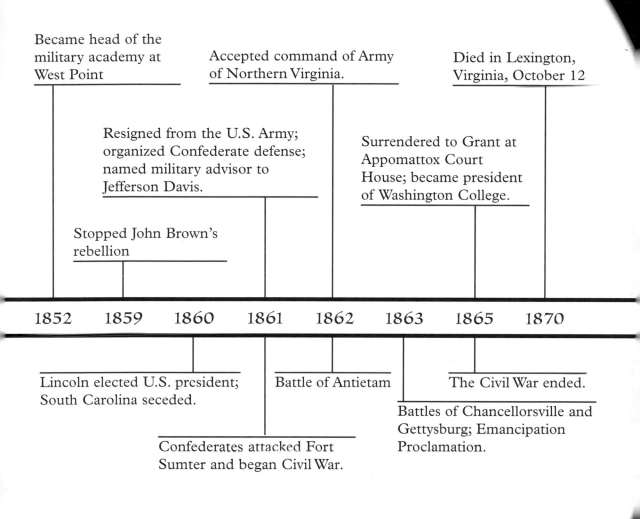

Became head of the military academy at West Point

Accepted command of Army of Northern Virginia.

Died in Lexington, Virginia, October 12

Resigned from the U.S. Army; organized Confederate defense; named military advisor to Jefferson Davis.

Surrendered to Grant at Appomattox Court House; became president of Washington College.

Stopped John Brown's rebellion

| 1852 | 1859 | 1860 | 1861 | 1862 | 1863 | 1865 | 1870 |

Lincoln elected U.S. president; South Carolina seceded.

Battle of Antietam

The Civil War ended.

Battles of Chancellorsville and Gettysburg; Emancipation Proclamation.

Confederates attacked Fort Sumter and began Civil War.

Glossary

arsenal (AR-suh-nuhl)—a military storehouse of guns and ammunition

cadet (kuh-DET)—a student at the U.S. Military Academy at West Point

cavalry (KAV-uhl-ree)—an army on horseback

Confederacy (kuhn-FED-ur-uh-see)—the 11 states that seceded from the Union: Alabama, Arkansas, Florida, Georgia, Louisiana, Mississippi, North Carolina, South Carolina, Tennessee, Texas, and Virginia

Emancipation Proclamation (i-man-si-PAY-shuhn prok-luh-MAY-shuhn)—Abraham Lincoln's order to free all slaves in Confederate-held territory; the Emancipation Proclamation took effect on January 1, 1863.

engineer (en-juh-NIHR)—a person who uses math and science to design roads, bridges, waterways

secede (si-SEED)—to withdraw formally from an organization; 11 Southern states seceded from the United States before the Civil War.

tuberculosis (tu-bur-kyuh-LOH-siss)—a disease that affects the lungs, making breathing difficult

Union (YOON-yuhn)—the states that remained loyal to the federal government during the Civil War; there were 23 Union states during the Civil War.

For Further Reading

Clinton, Catherine. *Scholastic Encyclopedia of the Civil War.* New York: Scholastic Reference, 1999.

Collier, Christopher, and James Lincoln Collier. *The Civil War 1860–1866.* Drama of American History. New York: Benchmark Books, 1998.

Graves, Kerry A. *The Civil War.* America Goes to War. Mankato, Minn.: Capstone Books, 2001.

Graves, Kerry A. *Going to School during the Civil War: The Confederacy.* Going to School in History. Mankato, Minn.: Blue Earth Books, 2002.

Hakim, Joy. *War, Terrible War.* History of US. New York: Oxford University Press, 1999.

Kerby, Mona. *Robert E. Lee: Southern Hero of the Civil War.* Historical American Biographies. Springfield, N.J.: Enslow Publishers, 1997.

Stanchak, John E. *Civil War.* DK Eyewitness Books. New York: Dorling Kindersley Publishers, 2000.

Places of Interest

Antietam National Battlefield
Sharpsburg, MD 21782
*http://www.nps.gov/anti/
contents.htm*
Site of Robert's first invasion of
the Union in Maryland

**Appomattox Court House
National Historic Park**
Highway 24
Appomattox, VA 24522
http://www.nps.gov/apco
Site of Robert's surrender
to Grant

**Arlington House:
The Robert E. Lee Memorial**
George Washington Memorial
Parkway
Turkey Run Park
McLean, VA 22101
*http://www.nps.gov/arho/
history.htm*
Robert's family home before the
war, now a national cemetery

**Gettysburg National
Military Park**
97 Taneytown Road
Gettysburg, PA 17325-2804
*http://www.nps.gov/gett/
home.htm*
Site of the turning point of the
Civil War

Lee Chapel
Washington and Lee University
Lexington, VA 24450
*http://www.lexingtonvirginia.com
/lee_chapel_and_museum.htm*
Chapel that Robert designed;
includes a museum about Robert

Stratford Hall Plantation
Stratford, VA 22558
http://www.stratfordhall.org
Birthplace of Robert E. Lee

U.S. Military Academy
West Point, NY 10996
*http://www.usma.army.mil/
guide_page/visiting.htm*
Robert E. Lee went to school and
was president here; Internet
address offers links to academy
information

Internet Sites

Do you want to learn more about Robert E. Lee?
Visit the FactHound at *www.facthound.com*

FactHound can track down many sites to help you. All the
FactHound sites are hand-selected by our editors. FactHound will
fetch the best, most accurate information to answer your questions.

IT'S EASY! IT'S FUN!
1) Go to *www.facthound.com*
2) Type in: **0736810897**
3) Click on **FETCH IT** and FactHound will put you on the trail
   of several helpful links.

You can also search by subject or book title. So, relax
and let our pal FactHound do the research for you!

Index